ODD ANIMALS OUT

WRITTEN BY
Ben Hoare

ILLUSTRATED BY
Asia Orlando

Author Ben Hoare
Illustrator Asia Orlando
Consultant Nick Crumpton
Senior Acquisitions Editor James Mitchem
Editor Abi Maxwell
US Editor Mindy Fichter
US Senior Editor Shannon Beatty
Senior Project Art Editor Charlotte Milner
Designers Sonny Flynn, Bettina Myklebust Stovne,
Brandie Tully-Scott
Managing Editor Jonathan Melmoth
Managing Art Editor Diane Peyton Jones
Production Editor Becky Fallowfield
Senior Production Controller Ena Matagic
Jacket and Sales Material Coordinator Elin Woosnam
Jacket Designer Charlotte Milner
Senior Picture Researcher Sakshi Saluja
Art Director Mabel Chan
Managing Director Sarah Larter

First American Edition, 2024
Published in the United States by DK Publishing
1745 Broadway, 20th Floor, New York, NY 10019

A CIP catalogue record for this book
is available from the British Library.
ISBN: 978-0-7440-9921-8

Printed and bound in China

www.dk.com

MIX
Paper | Supporting
responsible forestry
FSC™ C018179

This book was made with Forest
Stewardship Council™ certified
paper – one small step in DK's
commitment to a sustainable future.
Learn more at
www.dk.com/uk/information/sustainability

CONTENTS

INTRODUCTION

Some animals don't look or behave as we expect. They just do things differently than their relatives. These are the "rule breakers." Take sharks, for example. Everyone knows sharks are predators. So who would have thought one could actually be vegetarian? But it is!

Maverick animals like the veggie shark exist all over the planet. Their adaptations and lifestyles are often seriously bizarre. But whatever it is that makes them odd, these quirky creatures share something special. They became, or evolved, this way in order to survive.

Did you know there are walking fish? In this book, you will also meet a snake that can fly, kangaroos in trees, a spider that makes friends with a frog, wasps that make honey, and last but not least, a mouse that howls at the moon. Sometimes, it's good to be different.

Scientists discovered many of these "odd animals out" long ago. Other cases have only come to light recently. We have much still to learn about life on Earth, but one thing is certain—the natural world is full of surprises!

—BEN HOARE

SEA SNAKES

As strange as it sounds, some snakes live at sea. Found in the Indian and Pacific Oceans, they have flattened bodies to help them swim, and give birth to live babies underwater.

ECHIDNAS

The world has five species of mammals that lay tiny eggs instead of giving birth. Four are hedgehog-like animals called echidnas, and the other is the duck-billed platypus. All live in Australia.

PLATYPUS

IT'S GOOD TO BE DIFFERENT

We organize animals into groups, or families, of species with much in common. This branch of science is called taxonomy. However, many families include species that in some respects are different from the rest. They are rule breakers that stick out from the crowd.

KOMODO DRAGON

This is one of just three lizards with venom in its bite—the others are the Gila monster and the Mexican beaded lizard. On rare occasions, a female dragon reproduces without a male, a phenomenon called "virgin birth."

GILA MONSTER

MEXICAN BEADED LIZARD

COMMON POORWILL

Hibernation, a dormant state like deep sleep, is extremely unusual in birds. In fact, North America's common poorwill is the only one to do it! This behavior enables it to survive cold winters.

BAGWORMS

These are moths, not worms! However, their caterpillars do live in "bags"—camouflaged cases made from twigs, bark, or plant stems. Equally weird, most female bagworm moths are wingless, and some are legless, too.

THE CRAB AND THE ANEMONE

Sea anemones have stinging tentacles, like painful spaghetti, so other creatures steer clear. But a few species, such as the porcelain crab, are immune to the anemone's venom. The anemone's toxic tentacles give the crab somewhere safe to hide.

NARWHAL

The narwhal is a whale like no other. It has a single tooth—a giant canine that sticks out from its upper lip, like a unicorn horn. Normally, only males have this mysterious tusk, and scientists still debate its purpose.

MOUNTAIN MAGIC

Some of the slugs on Mount Kaputar, in Australia, look very odd indeed. Cut off from the rest of the world, they have turned into PINK giants that are 8 in (20 cm) long. Their neon coloration is a mystery. One theory is that it may be because of the lack of predators on top of the isolated peak—these slugs have no need to hide.

MOUNT KAPUTAR PINK SLUG

OUT OF PLACE

Animals tend to make their home in a particular habitat. Sometimes, however, they end up in different environments and adapt to suit their surroundings. From lizards at sea, to kangaroos in trees, these species live in all sorts of unexpected places.

VITAMIN SEA

Marine iguanas are the only sea-loving lizards on Earth. Found on the tropical Galápagos Islands, they sunbathe on black rocks to boost their body temperature. When energized, they dive into the glittering ocean to graze on nutritious green algae. These swimming lizards can hold their breath for at least 10 minutes!

MARINE IGUANA

GOLDEN MOLE

DESERT GOLD

At night, curious mammals with no eyes and silky fur the color of buttery toast scurry across African deserts. These are golden moles, and they move around by "swimming" through sand, just below the surface. Though we call them moles, their closest relatives include tenrecs (small mammals in Madagascar) and tiny elephant shrews.

LUMHOLTZ'S TREE-KANGAROO

Tree-kangaroos are called "teddy bears of the forest" due to their thick fur and round faces.

FOREST ACROBATS

Long ago, all kangaroos lived in trees. A few still do! These rainforest species, the tree-kangaroos, are found in New Guinea, Indonesia, and northern Australia. They can shift each back leg separately, unlike kangaroos that hop along the ground and have to move both legs together. This helps them climb far above the forest floor.

PECULIAR PENGUINS

Among the world's toughest birds, most penguins have to manage freezing conditions and snowstorms that rage for days. Most, but not all...

TOTALLY TROPICAL

Only five species of penguins actually breed in Antarctica. The rest live on coasts around the southern half of the world, where the ocean is still quite cold. However, there's one that swims through dazzling blue seas under a tropical Sun! The Galápagos penguin takes its name from a group of Pacific islands at the equator, which it shares with giant tortoises, seaweed-munching lizards, flamingos, and many other extraordinary animals.

GALÁPAGOS
PENGUIN

KEEPING IT COOL

Whereas most penguins face a constant battle to stay warm, the Galápagos penguin has the opposite problem: how to stop itself from overheating. So, it has fewer feathers and much less insulating fat than other penguins do. Panting like a dog is another of its tricks to cool down!

RAINFOREST PENGUINS

Penguins waddling through a rainforest? Sounds impossible, but it's true! The tawaki, or Fiordland crested penguin, nests among the tangled roots of huge old trees on the shores of New Zealand's South Island. This precious habitat is called temperate rainforest. It's extremely wet, but much cooler than any rainforest in the tropics.

The tawaki is one of the rarest penguins. Scientists think only 2,500–3,000 breeding pairs survive, but it's hard to be sure—their rainforests are so remote!

TAWAKI PENGUIN

CHILLED OUT

You can often smell and hear penguin breeding colonies long before you reach them. They are stinky places, packed with birds squabbling, honking, or braying like donkeys. The tawaki is different. It's quiet and shy, and each pair prefers to nest well away from their neighbors.

GOING UNDERGROUND

From time to time, scientists come across an animal so strange they are blown away. The mole-like purple frog—previously only known by the local people—is one such example.

PURPLE PATCH

The Western Ghats in India is a land of ancient mountains, much older than the Himalayas. It is a hotspot for unusual animals found nowhere else on the planet, but for weirdness, none of them come close to the purple frog. All its life, this pudgy amphibian hides in the damp mountain soil, only surfacing to breed.

Female frogs like this one are roughly three times the length of males.

After the first downpour, male frogs call the females out from underground.

The smaller males piggyback on the females, which are the larger size of squashed tennis balls.

LIFE IN EARTH

The purple frog's peculiar color is not even its oddest feature. For starters, it is flattened and lumpy, with a head that looks too small for its body. Its stumpy front legs are made for burrowing, but though muscular, can barely lift its saggy belly. And its snout is pointed like a pig—useful for sniffing out ant-like termites underground.

BIG NIGHT OUT

India's monsoon is a season of torrential rains. As water levels rise, turning streams to torrents, the purple frog is finally able to breed. The males and females venture above ground for one night only, mate in streams, then disappear again. Their tadpoles have sucker mouths to cling onto stones, otherwise the floodwater would wash them away.

BURROWING OWL

This owl breaks all the rules! It's active by day as well as night, and thanks to long legs, would rather run than fly. Not only that—it nests underground. The species lives in sandy plains where it can easily excavate a burrow, but prefers to renovate an old one that was previously dug by a tortoise or prairie dogs.

Having mated, each female lays several thousand eggs in a stream.

→

The frogs retreat back underground for another year.

WATER SURPRISE

Fresh and salt water are utterly different. Just ask anyone who has gulped a mouthful of seawater! Animals need special adaptations for each of these watery worlds, so it's rare to find species that survive in both.

COLOSSAL COUSINS

Ancient seas were full of fearsome reptiles, including monster crocodiles as long as double-decker buses. The last of those colossal crocs died out with the dinosaurs, but their descendants, saltwater crocodiles, still cruise the southeast Pacific Ocean. They are the world's largest living reptiles—some massive males reach more than 16 ft (5 m) from their scaly snouts to the tip of their mighty tails!

SALTWATER CROCODILE

READY SALTED

Saltwater crocs—Australians call them "salties"—are equally at home along coasts or in rivers and swamps. Boats have spotted them surfing waves way out in the open ocean. Moving between fresh water and the sea is usually dangerous for animals because it upsets the balance of salt in their bodies. However, salties get rid of any extra salt through glands in their huge tongues.

WATCH OUT!

Muscular and powerful, bull sharks are relatives of great white sharks. For years, scientists were baffled by their habit of swimming into estuaries and heading far upriver. Even shallow, murky water is no problem. We now know that, unlike any other sharks, bull sharks migrate between fresh and salt water, probably to feed or breed.

Bull sharks have been seen 2,300 miles (3,700 km) up the Amazon River in Peru. In Central America, they even enter lakes.

BULL SHARK

BAIKAL SEAL

In Russia, there are wild seals hundreds of miles from the nearest sea. Their home is Lake Baikal, the deepest and oldest lake on Earth, which holds over one-fifth of all fresh water on the surface of the planet. The ancestors of Baikal seals lived in the ocean long ago, and probably swam up rivers to reach the lake.

BUOYANCY AIDS

Argonauts may be the oddest octopuses on Earth. All other octopuses are totally naked, with their soft bodies on show. Female argonauts have spiral shells as thin as tissue paper. The beautiful shells are cases for their eggs, and fill with air so that the argonauts bob along near the surface of the ocean.

SHELLING OUT

Over millions of years, animals adapt to their environment. Their many adaptations are wonders of nature. For example, think about shells. The tough body armor is the first thing you notice about animals such as turtles and snails. But not all shells are alike...

BIG SOFTIES

Turtle shells are covered in hornlike plates. These offer excellent protection, yet the turtles can't breathe through them, which explains why some species lost theirs long ago. They replaced them with a leathery version they can breathe through, even underwater. The soft-shelled turtles also breathe through their snorkel-shaped mouths—and their bottoms!

THAT'S COOL

There is no mistaking the pink fairy armadillo—it is the only mammal with a pink shell! The structure has many flexible joints, like a lobster shell. Other armadillos use their shells for defense, but that is not what this one is for. The pink fairy armadillo pumps warm blood into it to cool down in the hot, sandy plains where it lives.

PINK FAIRY ARMADILLO

HERMIT CRAB

SHELL SUITS

Hermit crabs can no longer make shells of their own. They borrow them instead. When sea snails die, their empty shells are left behind, so all hermit crabs have to do is search for one the right size, then squeeze inside. When they grow too big for their adopted shell, they dump it and crawl away to find a replacement that fits.

17

GROWING UP

Amphibians lead double lives. They start life in fresh water, then transform into adults that hop, waddle, or creep around on land. The magical change they go through is "metamorphosis." But some have different ideas...

AXOLOTL

ODD BODS

Salamanders are long-tailed amphibians that people often mistake for lizards. Some of the oddest are axolotls, found in a single lake in Mexico. When they reach adulthood, you would expect them to crawl out of the lake to live in a forest or swamp, like other salamanders, but no. Instead, they spend their entire life in the same lake, slithering around the muddy bottom on stumpy little legs.

Axolotls always have broad grins on their faces! Their enormous "smiling" mouths are perfect for slurping worms.

GOOD AS NEW

Injuries can prove fatal for animals, but axolotls simply regrow missing or damaged body parts. Need a new leg? No problem. New tail? Easy. And that's not all. Axolotls can also replace their eyes, gills, and lungs, and repair parts of their brain. The new organs work perfectly, as if nothing had ever happened.

PARADOXICAL FROG

Parents are usually larger than their offspring. Not so with the paradoxical frog. Its tadpole is like any other to begin with, but then it grows and grows...until it is longer than a kitchen fork! The titanic tadpole shrinks to become a frog, ending up over three times smaller.

Egg

Larva

Larva, two legs

Adult

FOREVER YOUNG

Axolotls hatch from jellylike eggs laid in water—all totally normal for amphibians. Their larvae, the juvenile stage, are also quite normal. What happens next certainly isn't. As the larvae become adults, they keep their set of aquatic larval features. This includes their gills and the six feathery arms that enable them to breathe underwater. They may live for 10–15 years, but you could say axolotls never grow up.

WILD AXOLOTL

DIFFERENT COLORS

Most axolotls are baby pink—and if you think that's slightly odd, you're correct. They are bred in captivity to look like this. Wild axolotls are grayish-green with dark freckles, which is much better for hiding in their weedy lake. Since the species is critically endangered, there are now far more pink axolotls in tanks than naturally dark ones in Mexico.

YELLOW-SPOTTED SALAMANDER

GREEN FOR GO

Animals lack chlorophyll, the fabulous green stuff that enables plants to carry out photosynthesis. But what if they borrowed some? That's what the yellow-spotted salamander does. It lets algae live INSIDE its body, and these tiny green plants share the food they make. Corals in the sea do this, too, but the salamander is the only vertebrate able to pull it off.

WELCOME GUESTS

How does the salamander get its algae in the first place? In spring, the female lays her jellylike eggs in ponds, and the water is full of—you guessed it—algae. The algae soon enter the salamander embryos, turning the eggs bright green! Once inside, the microscopic guests stay put as the embryos turn into larvae.

SOLAR-POWERED

The sun is an amazing source of energy, and plants rely on it to survive. Sunlight powers the chemical reaction photosynthesis, by which plants make their food. And they're not alone...

ALGAE HUNTING

Several kinds of sea slugs can harness the sun's energy after chomping algae, and all of them are green. Most are weirdly shaggy or flat like leaves, because it increases their surface area to absorb more sunlight, which boosts the photosynthesis going on inside. The things that look like ears are sensitive organs called rhinophores, which help them find fresh supplies of algae.

Leaf sheep lay their eggs in a spiral shape, often counterclockwise.

LETTUCE SEA SLUG

LOOKING SHEEPISH

You can see how "leaf sheep" sea slugs got their nickname. Much like real sheep, these extraordinary creatures spend their time grazing, though they munch algae rather than grass. But they don't digest it entirely. They keep the special parts that contain chlorophyll, known as chloroplasts, and add them to their own tissues. Now the sneaky slugs are solar-powered!

"Leaf sheep" can only live in shallow water since they need plenty of sunlight.

LEAF SHEEP SEA SLUG

GIANT PANDA

GET A GRIP

Giant pandas eat bamboo, and a lot of it. (They have to, because it's not very nutritious.) Hang on, though. Surely there's a snag? Bear paws can't grip things! Of all mammals, only monkeys and apes can do that, thanks to thumbs that bend toward the fingers. But pandas are no ordinary bears. They in effect have a sixth digit on each of their front paws, which helps them pick things up.

FUNNY BONE

There's more to a giant panda's "extra digit" than meets the eye. It is not an actual digit, as it doesn't contain finger bones. In fact, it's an extension of a bone in the wrist. This false thumb cannot rotate like a human thumb, but it is strong and mobile enough to help the panda to eat virtually half its weight in bamboo each day.

ALL FINGERS AND THUMBS

We humans make do with four fingers and a thumb on each hand. But there are times when a different arrangement can be very—there's no better word for it—handy.

BROWN BEAR   GIANT PANDA

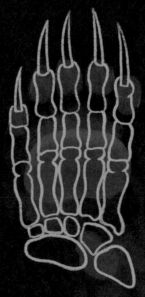
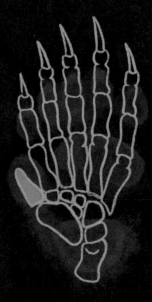

FREAKY FINGER

Mammals don't come any odder than the aye-aye. Everything about it is unusual... especially its fingers. The fourth one is massively long and skinny, almost like wire, and incredibly bendable. The aye-aye taps on trees with it, while listening for the hollow sound of beetle larvae tunnels under the bark. Then, it pokes out the juicy grubs.

AYE-AYE

Amazingly, the aye-aye is a primate. It belongs to Madagascar's lemur family.

THUMB

PSEUDO THUMB

RULE OF THUMB

The aye-aye keeps on surprising scientists. In 2019, researchers discovered it has a tiny extra thumb on the side of its palm that nobody had noticed before. The secret thumb is made from bone and cartilage, which is the softer material at the end of your nose. It gives the aye-aye a firm grip in the treetops, which the other bony fingers aren't very good at.

BLACK-AND-WHITE COLOBUS

Sometimes thumbs are a nuisance. If you're a monkey, they can get in the way when leaping from tree to tree, so Africa's black-and-white colobus basically does without them. Its thumbs are too small to be seen—it appears to have just four fingers on each hand. Being thumbless enables the colobus to move even faster through the forest.

CURIOUS COLORS

Birds are great show-offs. Their colorful plumage attracts mates or sends warning messages. But have you ever wondered why their feathers look the way they do? You might be surprised!

SUPER GREEN

Turacos are the only truly green birds in the world. While other birds, such as parrots, might appear green, they aren't really. Their feathers lack green pigment and just seem green due to how their surface reflects light.

NATURALLY FABULOUS

Birds mostly get their feather colors from pigments. These dye-like substances occur widely in the natural world. Some pigments, birds make for themselves, but others come from their diet. Flamingos, for instance, are only pink because of the shrimp and microscopic algae they eat. Turacos, pigeon-sized birds that live in African forests, have unusual pigments not found in any other bird—or indeed any other animal. The secret ingredient? Copper!

RED ALERT

Perched deep in a forest, turacos blend in with the surrounding greenery. When they fly, it's a different story. As their wings flick open, the flashes of red are dazzling. This probably helps catch the attention of other turacos—handy if there's a predator in the area and they need to make a quick exit.

People once thought a turaco's colors dissolve in the rain, but it's a myth!

COPPER BIRDS

Turacos love fruit and juicy young leaves, both rich in copper. The metal is absorbed by their bodies and is a vital part of two unique pigments. One, called turacoverdin, creates green feathers. The other, turacin, turns feathers red. The more fresh fruit and leaves these birds eat, the brighter their plumage.

WATERBERRIES

LIVINGSTONE'S TURACO

KERMODE BEAR

North America's black bears are famous for their sleek dark coats—except a few have creamy white fur, so look more like polar bears. Known as Kermode bears, they are not albino. Their ghostly coloration is a different type of inherited condition. Kermode bears live only in Great Bear Rainforest on Canada's west coast, where just a few hundred survive.

UNEXPECTED CARNIVORES

The members of each animal family normally have a similar diet. There are always exceptions, however! Here are some surprising creatures that have given up being vegetarian and turned carnivore.

TOOTHY BEES

Bees usually feed from flowers, but South American vulture bees are carnivores. While they do still visit rainforest blooms, they get most protein from meat, not pollen. These bees track down dead animals and slice into the rotting flesh with a toothlike structure not found in any other bees. Back at their nest, they store meaty morsels to feed their grubs.

GRASSHOPPER MOUSE

MIGHTY MOUSE

In the deserts of the USA and Mexico lives one of the most lethal rodents around. The grasshopper mouse looks like the kind of mouse you might see in a house or backyard. But wait...it hunts grasshoppers, other mice, and even scorpions, whose venom seems not to affect it. Equally bizarre, it defends its territory by howling at the night sky like a wolf!

CARNIVOROUS DUNG BEETLE

OFF WITH THEIR HEADS

Feces, poop, manure, dung...whatever you call it, dung beetles love it! This stinky diet suits thousands of dung beetle species worldwide, yet a handful have turned into full-time predators. One, in Central America, attacks millipedes, but it lacks the killing mouthparts of most predatory insects. So it cuts their heads off—using its own chisel-shaped head!

KEA

WATCH THAT BEAK

The last place you'd expect to find a parrot is the top of a mountain in New Zealand. Then again, the kea is a very unusual parrot. Thanks to a viciously sharp beak, this bird can feast on dead animals, including sheep and roadkill. The kea is sneaky, too—it frequently steals food from tourists, and it seems to enjoy pulling windshield wipers off cars.

BLOOD AND BONES

Drinking blood and chomping bones is the stuff of horror stories. On the other hand, blood and bones make excellent meals, packed with protein. You may be squeamish about the idea, but some animals can't wait to dive in...

BEARDED VULTURE

BONE BREAKERS

Vultures are nature's garbage collectors—they flock to dead bodies and clear them away by, um, eating them. But whereas other species squabble over the flesh, bearded vultures prefer bones—and the fattier the better. One of their favorite tricks is to soar into the sky with a nice thick bone, then drop it on rocks to smash it. This reveals the super-nutritious bone marrow inside.

VAMPIRE BAT

South America has bats that survive entirely on blood—the only mammals to do this. Unsurprisingly, they're called... vampire bats. Having found their target—often a deer, wild pig, or horse—they shave off a patch of fur with their razor-sharp incisor teeth. Next, they cut into the flesh and lap away. Their frothy spit numbs the pain so the victim feels nothing, and it also contains a substance that keeps the blood from flowing. Mmm.

VAMPIRE FINCH

Up to six vampire finches may sip the blood of a single booby. Amazingly, it doesn't appear to do any harm.

RED-FOOTED BOOBY

PECK AND SIP

Wolf Island is a lonely volcano, part of the Galápagos Islands. The little finches living in this incredibly dry and rocky place often struggle to find enough to eat. But boobies, a kind of seabird, also nest here—and are a lifesaver for the finches. Pecking the boobies' feathers makes them bleed. Now all the finches have to do is sip until full.

ONE OF A KIND

There are over 50,000 species of spiders, found almost everywhere on land, and occasionally in water. More are discovered every year, but so far, we have found only a single vegetarian spider. It's a small, green-and-brown species called *Bagheera kiplingi*. That's the name scientists use—it doesn't have one in English.

BAGHEERA KIPLINGI

PLANT-POWERED

Spiders and sharks are often seen as the ultimate predators, renowned for how fast they dispatch prey. Yet one or two follow a plant-based diet—some of the time, at least.

TREE-MENDOUS

Bagheera lives on acacia, or thorn trees, and nibbles lumps on the leafy twigs that are rich in fat and protein. Odd snack for a spider! The strange swellings are homes for stinging ants, which in return protect the trees. Little *Bagheera* is careful to keep out of their way! It jumps to the safety of nearby leaves and branches, building its nest away from the ants. But, once in a while, it receives a payback...ant larvae make a nice snack.

ABSOLUTELY GRAZY!

Vegetarian sharks...you have got to be kidding! Until 2007, this would indeed have been a joke, but not any more. That year, marine scientists found seagrass, which forms lush "lawns" on the seabed, in the stomach of bonnethead sharks. It was no accidental mouthful. Further research showed that these sharks could graze on the seagrass, like weird cows.

INTESTINE

THAT TAKES GUTS

Totally vegetarian animals need a special digestive system. Cows, for instance, own an amazing four-part stomach. What about bonnethead sharks? It turns out their insides are similar to sharks that eat nothing but meat, so they don't have the usual adaptations for digesting plants. Instead, they probably rely on friendly bacteria in their gut to break the seagrass down.

DRAKENSBERG CRAG LIZARD

Insects, birds, and bats are well-known pollinators, but what about reptiles? In South Africa, there's a plant that teams up with a veggie lizard. The Drakensberg crag lizard visits the little green flowers to sip their nectar and gets sticky pollen all over its nose, pollinating them.

Bonnethead sharks are smaller members of the hammerhead shark family.

BONNETHEAD SHARK

In the spring, the fish owl pounces on frogs that are busy breeding, and so make for easy prey. It's a nice change from all that salmon!

GIANT OF THE FAMILY

Blakiston's fish owl is named after the 19th-century explorer Thomas Blakiston. The size of a toddler, with wings as big as an eagle, it is the largest owl on Earth.

THE FISHING OWL

Most owls hunt mice and other small mammals, but not this one. It's huge, it's fluffy, it has tufts of feathers like floppy ears...and it absolutely loves salmon.

FISHING EXPEDITION

As night falls on the bitterly cold forest, the fish owl sits on a riverbank or a rock midstream, watching and waiting. When it spots a silvery movement in the water, it swoops to grab the salmon with a tremendous splash. The bird is noisy when it flies—unlike other owls, which are as silent as ghosts. But since the fish is underwater, it hears nothing.

Launch

Swoop

FROZEN FORESTS

This enormous fluffball lives in the snowy forests of northeast Russia, where bears, wolves, and tigers prowl. Though endangered and incredibly hard to find, the booming "boo-hoo" call of Blakiston's fish owl can give it away. This secretive bird is also found on the island of Hokkaido in northern Japan, where people once treated it as a god.

BLAKISTON'S FISH OWL

FISHING CAT

As a rule, cats detest bath time, so it's not every day you see one up to its belly in water. Meet Asia's fishing cat, which might resemble a large tabby but it has a secret weapon—webbed paws. After dark, it wades into ponds and swamps, ready to leap on fish and haul them ashore. A paw-some performance!

GETTING WET

Owls usually avoid water and hate the rain, because their soft feathers are not very waterproof. But the fish owl doesn't seem to mind, and plunges into icy rivers to catch its dinner. Sometimes, it even wades in the shallows. The soles of its feet are covered in spiny scales, somewhat like the spikes on running shoes, to help it grip onto slippery fish.

Seize

33

SWEET TOOTH

We're forever being told to eat plenty of fresh fruit. After all, it's a great source of sugary energy, and full of vitamins and minerals. Many animals, known as frugivores, hardly eat anything else. And some very unlikely species also have a sweet tooth.

HIGH-RISE

With their extremely long legs, maned wolves look like they're on stilts. In fact, they're the tallest members of the dog family. Why are they so tall? The answer is that their height is perfect for peering over long grass as they stride through the savannas of South America. Though mice are their main prey, up to half of their diet is fruit. No other wolf or fox eats as much of the sweet stuff.

MANED WOLF

BERRY SPECIAL

Maned wolves adore one berry above all others—the lobeira, which is like a fat, green tomato. In Brazil, people call it *fruta da lobo*, meaning "wolf fruit." When the berry is in season, the wolves gorge themselves silly, and in return do the lobeira plant a favor by scattering its seeds in their poop.

Wolf poops

Plant sprouts

Tree grows

PIRAPUTANGA

Rivers in the Amazon rainforest teem with fish. Meat-eating piranhas are surely the most well-known, but there's one that chows down on fruit—the piraputanga. It swims around, eyeing the juicy berries on branches overhanging the river, then rockets out of the water to snatch its prize. Later, the inedible seeds will be squirted out of its rear end, helping the trees to colonize new areas of forest.

COCONUT CRAB

Coconut crabs live on islands in the Indian and Pacific Oceans. Apart from munching coconuts, these mega-crabs also hunt BIRDS!

OUCH!

Coconuts look like nuts, but they are actually unusual fruit with tough shells. Believe it or not, there are crabs that make a meal of them. The giant crustaceans known as coconut crabs develop at sea before spending their adult lives on land. Not only can they climb trees, they are armed with massive, shell-crushing claws. Their pincers squeeze much harder than a human can—and could even crack your ribs.

HIDE AND SQUEAK

Southern Europe, Asia, and Africa are home to death's-head hawkmoths, named for the skull pattern behind their head. These large moths have a most unusual talent. If something disturbs them in their daytime hiding place, they SQUEAK. To make the surprising sound, they force air down their long tongue, inside which is a structure that vibrates, like the reed in a clarinet mouthpiece.

STRANGE SOUNDS

The animal world is full of sounds, which can be incredibly beautiful, downright strange, or sometimes a little annoying. Every now and again we come across species that sounds nothing like you might expect.

SUMATRAN RHINO

RARE PERFORMANCE

Sumatran rhinos have an amazing song— somewhere between a warble, a trill, and a moan. People often say it's like humpback whales singing! The sound travels great distances through the rhinos' rainforest habitat to help them communicate. Sadly, as the species is critically endangered, there are hardly any rhinos left to sing in reply.

TOKAY GECKO

LOUD AND LONG

Weird chatter echoes through the night in Southeast Asia. It is produced by tokay geckos, and sounds like someone saying "TO-KAY, TO-KAY, TO-KAY" over and over. The nocturnal lizard chorus is so loud and repetitive, it can make people quite irritated!

The way tenrecs produce sound is called stridulation. They are the only mammals able to do it.

RATTLE AND STRUM

Madagascar has little mammals that look like hedgehogs and behave like hedgehogs, but aren't hedgehogs. They are streaked tenrecs. Their bodies are covered in hundreds of spines—actually sharp hairs—which they rub together to make scratchy rattles and squeaks. The sound is too high-pitched for human ears, but other tenrecs still hear it.

STREAKED TENREC

37

CAVE TALK

Getting around in the dark is tricky. Nocturnal animals have specially adapted eyes, but even they can't see in absolute darkness. There has to be a better way...

CLICK TRICK

If a pigeon was to swoop around in a pitch-black cave, it would end badly. Even owls would struggle. So how does the oilbird–which looks like a cross between an owl and a swallow, and nests in rainforest caverns–avoid crashing? Its secret is that it "sees" with sound. This unique bird produces clicks and listens for the echoes of its own voice to learn where everything is.

OILBIRD

BAT BIRD

The oilbird's amazing sensory system, echolocation, is also used by bats. But whereas bat squeaks are too high-pitched for us to hear, its deeper clicks are within human hearing. The "bat bird" has borrowed an idea from mammals, too: whiskers. Its stiff facial hairs feel whatever is nearby, including other oilbirds in the busy cave colony.

TWO TRIBES

Underground pools are an unusual habitat for fish, but Mexican tetras get along fine in flooded caves that never see daylight. Some tetras also live at the surface, and these fish are stunningly different to those in the dark caves. Those deep underground are now eyeless! The blind fish make sharp clicks as they patrol their dark pools, and use the returning ripples to map out their surroundings.

Cave animals like the tetras are often ghostly pale. There's no need for bright colors in an always-dark world.

MEXICAN TETRA

ENERGY SAVING

Scales grow over the empty eye sockets of the Mexican tetras. This may seem a bit spooky, but doing without vision makes sense. Eyes are complex organs, so they take a lot of energy to grow and maintain. As food supplies are limited in cave pools, it's better for these fish to save precious resources to power body parts that will be of more use.

COMMON SHREW

Shrews are hyperactive little mammals that chirp and cheep. They are not just chatting—it actually stops them from bumping into things during their night-time explorations. At close range, the sounds bounce off objects, like a simple form of echolocation.

FUNNY HONEY

Gloopy, golden, gorgeous—it's got to be honey!
This sweet substance is, of course, made by honeybees.
Yet they're not the only ones who produce it. A few
other bees do, too, as do several other insects.

Honey wasps live
in Central and South
America. Some say their
honey tastes like
maple syrup.

FLOWER POWER

Wasps have a bad reputation, which
is REALLY unfair because they're a
vital part of the natural world.
Some species even make honey!
Called honey wasps, they suck up
sugary nectar from flowers
and return to their nest
to convert it to honey.
Just like honeybees,
they store it to
feed the colony
when other food
is hard to find.

MEXICAN HONEY WASP

HONEYBEE

HAIRY TALE

Honey wasp honey is much the same as
honeybee honey. It's a great source of
energy, full of fructose and glucose,
which are kinds of sugar. As the wasps
fly from flower to flower gathering the
nectar, they pollinate the blooms. Their
hairy bodies help the pollen stick, so they
look more "bee" than "wasp."

HOME SWEET HOME

Honey wasps construct beautiful nests, but while bees use wax as a building material, wasps prefer paper. They make their nests from wood sliced from trees in thousands of tiny strips. Their scissorlike jaws cut slivers of wood off tree trunks, and they chew the wood, mixing it with saliva to make a pulp. Back at the nest site, the mixture hardens as it dries, forming thin, gray paper.

The paper is used to make individual cells for eggs and larvae, as well as the exterior of the nest.

WASP NEST

The finished nest hangs from a branch in the treetops of their tropical forest home.

HONEYPOT ANT

These quirky ants carry nectar down to their nests in Australian deserts, where they feed it to special storage ants until their bellies are almost bursting. These storage ants hang like living jars of honey. Whenever any of the colony need a meal, the storage ants bring the honey right back up for them. Sweet!

41

NIGHT MONKEY

When the sun goes down, night monkeys know it's time to get up. They set off to explore the moonlit forest, while other monkeys snuggle together and snooze.

STRONG BONDS

Night monkeys live in small families made up of a breeding pair and up to four young of different ages. The parents are devoted partners, which in other monkey species is unheard of. To mark their territory, the couple urinates on their hands and feet! It means they leave smelly trails through the treetops.

A night monkey father carries his baby...

plays with it...

KĀKĀPŌ

As well as being one of very few nocturnal parrots, New Zealand's kākāpō holds many records. It is the world's heaviest parrot, the only one unable to fly, and the only one where males compete at display arenas to attract females. What's more, its plumage looks like moss, and smells of honey and old wood!

PROUD FATHERS

With night monkeys, it is mostly fathers that look after the young. Mothers suckle their infants, but then hand them straight back—the dads are in charge of childcare. It is rare for mammals to be such dedicated dads, and that is especially true of primates.

grooms its fur...

and shows it how to pick the tastiest fruit.

WHAT A HOOT

These are the world's only nocturnal monkeys. Enormous, owl-like eyes allow them to find their way around the trees as if it were daylight. They don't just look like owls, but sound like them, too. Their hoots echo through the forest to show which area belongs to them. As dawn breaks, each family finds a tree hole to sleep in.

There are 11 species of night monkeys, all in South America. Most are the size of squirrels.

NIGHT MONKEY

THE GREAT ESCAPE

We talk about being "afraid of the dark," but for little monkeys like these, the hours of daylight are more dangerous. This is when eagles and hawks are on the hunt. Maybe night monkeys switched to a nocturnal life to escape such daytime predators? Or it might have been to avoid competing for food with other monkeys active during the day.

PROUD PARENTS

Looking after youngsters is hard work, as any human parent will tell you. Insects definitely think so, because most don't bother! They just lay their eggs and disappear, meaning they never even see their offspring. There are exceptions, though.

DEVOTED MOM

Unusually for a bug, the parent bug takes great care of its young. Well, the female does anyway. She is an attentive mother who lays her eggs under a tree leaf, then shields the cluster of tiny blobs for several days until they hatch. Her devotion protects them from attacks by parasitic wasps.

We have discovered more than a million species of insects so far, and just one percent of them look after their young.

PARENT BUG

SNUG AS BUGS

What about the male parent bug? He's much smaller than his partner and dies soon after mating, his job done. Meanwhile, the female sticks close beside her precious buglets—known as nymphs—for several weeks while they grow. Eventually, they turn into adult bugs and can fend for themselves.

GUARD DUTY

Earwigs are best known for the weird "pincers" at the end of their bodies, yet the most intriguing thing about them is their childcare arrangements. The female not only guards her nest in the soil, she frequently licks her eggs clean to give them a better chance of hatching. If the eggs are scattered–by a burrowing mole, say–the earwig mom stands her ground and gathers them up again.

EARWIG

SNACK TIME

After hatching, the young earwigs stay in the nest. They know that Mom is likely to bring them some pieces of rotting plant or animal from an expedition above ground. If they're lucky, she might vomit up some semi-digested food for dessert. This kind of tender care is incredibly rare in insects.

PIGEON

Have you ever seen a baby pigeon, or squab, stuff its scrawny head into a parent's beak? If so, you might have wondered what was going on. Amazingly, it was suckling! Pigeons are the only birds that suckle their chicks. Mother and father pigeons both offer a whitish fluid, known as pigeon milk, which comes from their crop, a part of the digestive system.

WALLACE'S FLYING FROG

FABULOUS FEET

Wallace's flying frog can soar through the rainforest trees, far above the ground. There are massive webs of skin between its toes. When it jumps off a tree, it spreads its feet to make four parachutes, which slow its descent into a graceful glide.

PARADISE TREE SNAKE

The paradise tree snake could glide from one end of a tennis court to the other.

GOING FULL SPEED

Amazingly, the paradise tree snake is able to glide between trees, despite not having limbs or flying membranes. After sliding to the end of a branch, it launches into space, holding itself flat like a ribbon. To keep going, it ripples its body into "S" shapes, as if swimming through air.

UP, UP, AND AWAY

A lack of wings has not stopped some unlikely animals from taking to the skies. In rainforests, there are lizards, frogs, and snakes that sail from tree to tree, and even a few fish have joined the flying club.

DRACO LIZARD

BOLT FROM THE BLUE

If you spot fish above the waves, you're not dreaming...flying fish actually take off! They rocket out of the sea to escape predators such as tuna, waggling their tail rapidly to propel themselves low over the water. Enormous pectoral fins open at the front of their body to keep them aloft for up to 45 seconds.

FLYING FISH

GETAWAY GLIDE

The Draco lizard has a head for heights, which is just as well, because it lives in the treetops. Running down a trunk to reach the next tree would take too long, especially when being chased by an enemy. Instead, it glides across. Huge membranes on each side of its body serve as "wings."

GROUNDED!

What's that snuffling in the undergrowth? A hedgehog, perhaps? In New Zealand, it could be a bat! Of all the world's bats, this one spends the least time flying.

BAT HABITS

Among mammals, only bats can truly fly like birds. And they make full use of their superpower. The lesser short-tailed bat, which lives in ancient forests, also flies. It just seems rather reluctant! Often, it prefers to scramble over the forest floor in search of crickets and other tasty insects, as well as fallen fruit and seeds.

The lesser short-tailed bat loves to lap nectar from the wood rose, a peculiar plant that looks as if it's made of bark.

When chasing moths, the bat stays close to the ground. At the end of the night, it flies to an old tree to roost.

To snag beetles and worms, the bat pushes its snout into piles of dead leaves.

GROUND WOODPECKER

There are more rocks than trees where the South African ground woodpecker lives. Unlike a typical woodpecker, this pink-and-gray bird gets around by hopping from boulder to boulder. It lives on ants, and travels around the hillside in small groups that stay in touch with loud cries.

WALK THIS WAY

Wings are not made for walking. So the lesser short-tailed bat has developed a clever way of folding them away and shuffling on its wrists instead. Awkward...but it works. The bat's back legs have also become much stronger—other bats only use them as hooks to hang from while they roost.

Bats are called *pekapeka* in New Zealand's Maori language. The country has just two species today.

LESSER SHORT-TAILED BAT

These bats typically spend 40 percent of their time feeding on plants. The rest is split between hunting insects on the ground and in the air.

EVOLUTION STORY

Why would bats wrist-walk rather than swoop through the night sky? It's because New Zealand has no other native mammals—and no snakes. Without predators, walking bats could forage on the ground in peace for millions of years. Unfortunately, humans introduced stoats, cats, and rats to the island nation. Walking bats are easy prey, so conservationists are creating predator-free zones to save them.

FLIGHTLESS BIRDS

Birds make flying look effortless. In fact, they work as hard as athletes to stay in the air-flight requires huge pectoral muscles and burns a lot of energy. No wonder some birds have given up.

FULL STEAM AHEAD

The southernmost shores of South America are a remote, rocky wilderness. Here, you will find ducks that, like the ostrich and emu, have long since lost the ability to fly. As they dash across the sea using their stubby wings as paddles, there's so much splashing you might think they're injured. Their paddling style reminded people of paddle steamer boats, so they're called steamer ducks.

DUCKING AND DIVING

Steamer ducks dive for crustaceans such as limpets. Their entire lives are spent on the same short stretch of seaweedy coast-after all, they're not flying anywhere! Steamer ducks are chunky-heavier than most geese-and overprotective parents. Any animal that ventures too close to their chicks, whether a playful penguin or a blubbery seal, is angrily chased away.

KAGU

If scientists come across a bird that's unlike any other, they place it in a family of its own. The kagu, which can barely fly, is one such bird, with no close relatives. It lives on the New Caledonia islands in the Pacific Ocean, and has the legs of a heron, the body of a chicken, and the head of a pigeon. When partners meet, they unfurl a punky crest to impress each other.

Though the takahē looks fierce, it nibbles plants and seeds. It eats for up to 19 hours a day!

GRASSLAND GIANT

Giving up flight has enabled New Zealand's takahē to become enormous. With its monster bill, this colorful bird has the appearance of a dinosaur! It's far heavier than any of its cousins, the moorhens and coots found on park lakes and in wetlands worldwide. But, while the takahē can't stay airborne on its stumpy wings, they do help it scramble up grassy slopes, along with its strong legs for running.

GOOD NEWS

The takahē was long thought extinct. In 1948, a tiny population was found safe and sound in the middle of nowhere in the Murchison Mountains. The discovery caused a sensation and led to a huge conservation project to rescue the species. Some have been bred in captivity and released in new areas to boost numbers in the wild, which have reached close to 500 birds.

JAPANESE MACAQUES

AND RELAX...

Japanese macaques live farther north than all other wild monkeys, and have thick fur to handle the severe winters. Even so, the bitter cold is a challenge. However, some of these monkeys have learned how to beat the winter blues. They bathe in volcanic springs where the water is 104°F (40°C). Groups of them soak in the steaming pools, as if lazing in a hot tub.

TAKING THE PLUNGE

Some unexpected animals spend time in water. And, as we shall see later, there are astonishing cases of animals normally found in fresh water habitats moving around on land.

EUROPEAN RAFT SPIDER

POND GIRL

Spiders generally don't enjoy getting their eight legs wet, but Europe's raft spider lives on ponds! The female, who is larger and more powerful than the male, floats her legs on the surface to feel the ripples made by prey. Alerted by the vibrations, she skates across to snatch her meal, usually an insect, tadpole, or small fish. Or she dives in to grab it—she can stay under for 20 minutes.

BUBBLE BLOWER

Though moles are built for digging, these expert tunnelers can also swim a short way. Yet only one, the star-nosed mole of North America, frequently takes a dip. It has a unique hunting technique in bogs and swamps. The mole blows bubbles through its nose into the water, and sniffs them back up to detect the scent of prey.

The star-nosed mole senses prey with the twitching pink "star" on its face.

STAR-NOSED MOLE

ADULT SNOUT MOTH

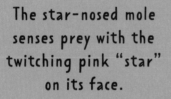

WATER-PILLAR

Unlikely as it sounds, some moths start life in... ponds. The female snout moths dip in the water to lay their eggs, or swim to the bottom. The caterpillars are perfectly happy underwater-they breathe through gills or their skin, or fold leaves to trap bubbles of air. After several months, they emerge at the surface as adult moths.

SNOUT MOTH CATERPILLAR

FISH OUT OF WATER

Fish are able to breathe underwater thanks to their gills. It's part of what makes a fish a fish. Yet a handful of remarkable species can also breathe air at the surface or on land, so they get the best of both worlds.

AIR GUZZLER

The northern snakehead is an adaptable fish. Much of the time, it breathes with its gills. But it also has a pair of special chambers, the suprabranchial organs, to gulp oxygen directly from the air. As a result, it happily survives in murky rivers and swamps where the water's oxygen levels get dangerously low.

A WRIGGLY WALK

Young northern snakeheads can squirm onto land–an incredible sight. The feat enables them to travel cross-country to different rivers or wetlands. Their bodies produce masses of slime to avoid drying out during their epic wrigglathon, and they mostly migrate in the cool of night, which helps, too.

A baby snakehead slithers over muddy ground with surprising ease. To propel itself, the fish makes "C" shapes with its long, flexible body.

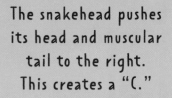

The snakehead pushes its head and muscular tail to the right. This creates a "C."

A snakehead can survive on land for up to four days.

FISHY BUSINESS

Northern snakeheads are powerful predators, with toothy jaws that mean business. In their natural home—China and other parts of East Asia—their aggressive appetite is no problem. They belong here. However, the python lookalikes have escaped into North America, where they eat all kinds of local wildlife. Because of the havoc they cause, the species has been nicknamed "fishzilla."

NORTHERN SNAKEHEAD

LUNGFISH

This wonderful fish has changed little from what its ancestors looked like nearly 400 million years ago. As its name suggests, it uses a pair of air-breathing lungs. That's not all. If the swamps it lives in dry up, it just burrows in the mud, makes a slimy sleeping bag for itself and waits, for weeks or even months, for the waters to return. Early scientists were left stumped—they thought this oddity must be a reptile or an amphibian.

Next it curves its head and tail to the left, which forms a reverse "C." It repeats these movements over and over.

SURF'S UP

Mastering the ocean waves takes time. It's not for everyone, but you never know until you give it a try. Where there's a will, there's a wave...

LIFE ON THE BEACH

Africa's rivers and swamps are the domain of the hippopotamus, whose name comes from two ancient Greek words meaning "horse" and "river," so it's a shock to see hippos surfing in the ocean! These extraordinary scenes occur on the coast of Gabon in West Africa. Perhaps the salt and spray kill pesky parasites on the hippos' smooth skin, or maybe, like humans, they simply enjoy it.

HIPPOPOTAMUS

On the same coast, you can see forest elephants stroll along the sand and paddle in the surf!

GOING UNDER

The typical view of a hippo is the top of a mighty head as it wallows in mucky brown water. Its nostrils, eyes, and ears are so high up, it can breathe and stay alert while almost fully submerged. This huge creature is too heavy to float and is unable to swim underwater, so it gallops along the muddy bottom of the riverbed, in a kind of bouncy ballet.

THE BIG BLUE

Earth, in many ways, is ruled by insects. Vast numbers flourish all over the planet...apart from in oceans. That's because insect bodies, especially their breathing systems, are built for life on land or in fresh water. Just five species, called sea skaters, survive permanently offshore. They scoot across the waves on skinny legs and pick tiny morsels of food off the surface.

SEA SKATERS

EGGS-TRA SPECIAL

Sea skaters, like most insects, lay eggs. But how can they possibly do that at sea? These specialized bugs have found a way–they use floating debris, such as feathers molted by passing seabirds! Today, tiny pieces of plastic will do, too. Sea skaters are among the few species to benefit from plastic pollution, which threatens so many marine animals.

PADDLING PIGS

Pigs dog-paddling in the sea? You bet! They have become a tourist attraction in the Bahamas, after a video of them went viral. These pigs are descended from a handful of hogs living on a remote island, which learned to jump in and swim to their owners' boats as they brought them food.

WALKING UNDERWATER

Incredible as it sounds, there are birds and fish that walk underwater. For their relatives, a stroll along the bottom would be out of the question.

HOLD TIGHT

Bubbling mountain streams have plenty of insects to eat–if you can get to them. Dippers, which are plump birds the size of thrushes, just walk to the water's edge and continue on, seeming to vanish under the surface. As they explore the streambed for prey, their strong claws grip stones to prevent them from floating back up.

COELACANTH

This deep-sea fish (you say its name "see-luh-kanth") has odd fins that stick out like training wheels on a child's bike. They resemble stumpy limbs, so they must be for walking...or so we thought. Scientists discovered that the coelacanth swims with them, but strangely for a fish, they move in pairs, much like a lizard or crocodile walks.

GOGGLE VISION

Dippers beat their wings to fight the current and propel themselves down. It's like flying while walking–but underwater, of course. To protect their eyes, see-through covers called nictitating membranes slide across like goggles. Another membrane closes their nostrils before they jump in. The birds also waterproof their feathers with oil from a special gland.

DIPPER

SEABED SHUFFLE

Tropical coral reefs support a dazzling array of fish, including several known as stonefish. These fish are able to lift their bodies off the seabed using the pectoral fins at their sides. Think of it as the fish version of a push-up! Once in this position, the stonefish do a sort of slow-motion shuffle across the sand.

STONEFISH

SPINES

WATCH OUT!

With their downturned mouths, stonefish are contenders for the world's grumpiest fish. Their jaws snap open to reveal ferocious teeth and gulp prey at lightning speed. That's not all—spines on their backs are loaded with venom said to be more powerful than in any other fish. Anyone who steps on a stonefish will definitely regret it!

SECURITY GUARD

The pistol shrimp welcomes a small fish called the shrimp goby into its burrow on the seabed. The fishy friend has superb eyesight. Whenever it spots a predator, it gives the shrimp a quick nudge with one of its fins, and both fish and shrimp dash inside to safety. The shrimp goby gets free lodging in return for its services.

PISTOL SHRIMP AND SHRIMP GOBY

ODD COUPLES

Once in a while, two species that have little in common manage to share the same living space. There can be advantages to getting along!

TERMITES

CASTLES OF CLAY

Termites are small insects, yet their nests are massive, as they live in colonies of thousands. Their nest mounds are built from dried earth and baked hard in the tropical Sun. Many other animals also use their nests, even while the termites are still there. Australia's buff-breasted paradise kingfisher is one of several birds that does this.

BUFF-BREASTED PARADISE KINGFISHER

TUATARA

Tuataras look like lizards—but aren't. Their closest cousins died out with the dinosaurs.

AWKWARD HOUSEMATES

Burrows can be in short supply on islands, and that means sharing is a tempting idea. Tuataras, a species of New Zealand reptile, move in with seabirds called fairy prions. But it seems the tuataras do better from this arrangement than the birds do. The burrows keep them warm at night, whereas the poor prions may end up with their eggs and chicks being eaten.

DWARF MONGOOSE

SWEET DREAMS

Africa's dwarf mongooses have many enemies, from eagles and hawks to venomous snakes. If their lookout spots danger, it sounds the alarm and the whole pack races for cover. Termite nest mounds make ideal hiding places. Often, packs sleep there, too. A large mound can accommodate a dozen or more dozing mongooses.

THE SLOTH AND THE MOTHS

Animals can have so many things living on them—
their body is an entire ecosystem. Think that's gross?
They sometimes do very well because of it.

MOBILE HOME

The three-toed sloth lives high up in trees in the rainforests of Central and South America. Its shaggy fur teems with other species. So much so, this slow-moving mammal is a complete hairy ecosystem. There are algae, fungi, and several kinds of moths, for which the sloth is their only home. The moths survive on traces of water and nutrients sucked off their host's skin.

2. Female sloth moths crawl off their host to lay their eggs in the fresh dung.

3. After the larvae hatch, and feed on the dung, they pupate into adult moths.

CALL OF NATURE

About once a week, the sloth descends to the forest floor to deposit its dung. Weird! Why use valuable energy to climb down and risk attack by predators? Part of the answer to this puzzle is that sloth moths lay their eggs in these poop piles, so they depend on this strange toilet routine. What about the sloth, though? Does it benefit? We now know it probably does...

1. A sloth digs a hole at the base of a tree and deposits its weekly dollop of dung.

BENEFITS ALL ROUND

Scientists think sloth moths help their furry host in two ways. First, they somehow fertilize its fur, perhaps by bringing nutrients from the dung left on the ground. This makes more algae grow, which turns the fur green, giving the sloth useful camouflage among the trees. Second, the sloth actually eats the algae. The algae is more nutritious than the leaves it eats!

THREE-TOED SLOTH

SLOTH MOTH

THE WHALE AND THE BARNACLES

Most barnacles cling to seashore rocks, thanks to a protein glue they produce that forms a bond as strong as cement. But some barnacles travel the oceans attached to the thick skin of whales, and don't live anywhere else. A gray whale can be carrying 330 lb (150 kg) of whale barnacles on its head and back!

Researchers once counted 120 sloth moths living on a single three-toed sloth.

63

IN GOOD COMPANY

Africa's naked mole rat is fabulously weird. It is peculiar for many reasons, but most of all for living in colonies like a social insect.

QUEEN OF IT ALL

A colony of naked mole rats has up to 300 members, ruled by a single breeding female-the queen. The rest are workers that dig tunnels and find food, or soldiers that defend the colony. When the queen dies, other females fight to the death to become the new queen. This lifestyle, called eusocial behavior, is shared with ants, termites, and honeybees. Mole rats are the only mammals that do it!

TUNNEL TOWN

Naked mole rats live in tunnels, and each colony can cover an area the size of a soccer field. Since it's always warm underground, mole rats don't need fur. And as they get around by smell, they are sightless, too-their eyes are tiny, like black dots. The mole rats scurry along their tunnels hunting for roots, bulbs, and other plant food, and they can reverse just as fast as they travel forward.

The workers

Soldier

NAKED MOLE RAT

NEWBORN PUPS

Naked mole rats have teeth in front of their lips, so they can dig with their mouths closed to stop dirt getting in.

PUPS

Incredibly, the queen mole rat has a new litter every 80 days, and they're huge! One queen gave birth to 27 pups–the largest-known litter of any mammal. Mole rats can live for more than 30 years, an astonishing age for a small rodent. They never get seriously ill, so scientists are studying them to discover their secret.

The queen

LION

Among the world's big cats, only lions seek company. They live in extended families called prides. Other big cat species are natural loners, unless breeding or raising cubs. Teamwork enables lions to hunt larger prey, such as zebras and buffalo, and makes it easier to defend their territory and young.

LITTLE AND LARGE

In the forests of South America, the dotted humming frog lives with a tarantula that towers over it. The frog preys on tiny insects attracted to leftovers of the spider's meals, and gains a huge, hairy bodyguard. In return, it pays "rent" by making itself useful. It eats the ants that would otherwise feast on the spider's eggs. Frog and tarantula both win!

HOME HELP

Nests quickly become messy, and dirt allows disease and parasites to thrive. To keep living quarters clean and tidy, some animals bring in other animals to help out.

PERUVIAN TARANTULA

DOTTED HUMMING FROG

TOYING WITH DEATH

Ordinarily, you would expect a little frog to be a goner if it met one of the planet's biggest spiders. So what is going on here? Scientists believe the tarantula is able to recognize this helpful species of frog and chooses to leave it unharmed. Probably, it identifies chemicals in the frog's skin, like a kind of signature.

SNAKES ALIVE!

In Texas, the eastern screech owl fetches snakes and drops them, still alive and wriggling, inside its tree-hole nest. The snakes are only small, so they're not interested in making a meal of the fluffy owl chicks. But they do snack on a variety of unwelcome nest guests, including mites and insects. Their hard work leaves the place spick-and-span!

EASTERN SCREECH OWL

Blind snakes look more like worms, and though minuscule, can swallow prey bigger than their head!

TEXAS BLIND SNAKE

PEST CONTROL

The blind snakes that help eastern screech owls would usually burrow through soil to hunt insect larvae. Once in an owl nest, they love to rummage around and keep the number of pests down. The owlets in the nest are much healthier as a result, and more likely to develop successfully.

TONGUE-TIED

Oceans swarm with crustaceans called isopods. Many are parasites, but just one of them is a tongue eater. It cuts off the blood supply to a fish's tongue, so the tongue shrivels up and falls off. The isopod stays attached...and the fish starts using it as a tongue instead! It is the only animal on Earth that replaces the body part of another animal.

TONGUE-EATING LOUSE ON A CLOWN FISH

COOKIECUTTER SHARK

CUT AND RUN

One shark behaves like a parasite-the cookiecutter. It is only the size of a bowling pin, but its bite is brutal. At night, it swims up to large fish-often other sharks-and latches on with strong lips. Still holding on, it spins around so its teeth tear off a chunk of flesh. The bite mark looks like it was made by a cookie cutter in dough.

PESKY PARASITES

Parasites live off other species, often by stealing their food, sucking their blood, or eating their host's tissues. To get away with it, they deploy all kinds of tricks. There are some weird and devious parasites out there!

Greenland sharks don't hunt by eyesight, so eye-eating parasites are no problem.

WHAT AN EYEFUL

Greenland sharks cruise slowly through the icy Arctic Ocean. They can live 400 years-longer than any other fish, reptile, amphibian, bird, or mammal. And, for most of their long and slow life, these huge sharks can't see. The cause? Parasites that dine on their eyeballs! The eye-munchers are unusual copepods, a type of crustacean.

LAMPREY

VAMPIRE FISH

Picture a muscular tube with a head at one end, and you have a good idea what a lamprey looks like. This fish has no jaws or backbone, and just a couple of simple fins, but its mouth is something else. Though jawless, the circular opening is packed with rings of hooked teeth. The lamprey uses it to clamp onto larger fish and drink their blood.

PARASITIC COPEPOD ON A GREENLAND SHARK

STOP, THIEF!

Dewdrop spiders are seriously tiny—smaller than a pea. This helps them slip into the webs of orb-web spiders undetected. They lurk at the edge, waiting to snatch bugs that get trapped. It's dangerous, but they get out of spinning their own webs. Plus, the webs they hang out in are bigger than any they could ever make, so better at catching prey.

ORB-WEB SPIDER

CATCH ME IF YOU CAN

If the orb-web spiders discover the thieves in their webs, they may kill them. To avoid detection, dewdrop spiders sometimes create a small web connected to the main one. This gives them a way of moving around secretly without bumping into their hosts. It's as if the two species of spiders are playing a deadly game of hide and seek...

LOSING OUT?

When they are robbed, the orb-web spiders lose out on food. The silk in their webs may also be torn or eaten by the dewdrop spiders. But the insects that the uninvited guests steal are usually too small for the orb-web spiders to bother with anyway. So, it could be that the rightful owners of the webs are no worse off.

A banana spider, a type of orb-web spider, sits in her freshly made web, unaware she is sharing it with a dewdrop spider.

When a morpho butterfly flies into the web, the banana spider grabs it. The dewdrop spider bides its time... this meal is far too big!

70

DEWDROP SPIDER

Dewdrop spiders live all over the world, but especially in the tropics.

HIGHWAYMAN FLY

This fly is a thief, too. Its fiendish strategy is to look for ant colonies moving to new nest sites. Suddenly, the fly attacks the lines of ants. During a hijack, it takes one of the eggs, larvae, or pupae (the cases in which larvae develop into adults) that the ants are carrying, and enjoys the tasty meal.

FOOD THIEVES

A few sneaky spiders have turned to a life of crime. They expertly steal the meals of their much larger cousins! Quite a risky move when you are robbing from killers with fangs full of venom.

A fly gets tangled in the web. The banana spider is busy, so the thief seizes its chance.

ABSENT PARENTS

One way to dodge the hard work of parenting is to get another species to take care of your young. We call these animals brood parasites, or "cuckoos."

CUCKOO BUMBLEBEE LARVAE

WORKER BUMBLEBEES

BUMBLEBEE LARVAE

NEST INVADERS

Female cuckoo bumblebees look and smell just like the queens of different bumblebees. This disguise enables them to muscle into nests of the other species. The intruders seize control from the true queens and usually sting them to death. Next, they lay their own eggs in the stolen nests and force the worker bumblebees to look after them instead.

Cuckoo bumblebees lack "baskets" for carrying pollen on their back legs, as other bees feed their larvae for them.

PLAN BEE

A female cuckoo bumblebee needs to plan her nest takeover carefully. She must attack a nest that is exactly the right size, with a suitable number of female workers. If there are too many, they may rebel and overpower her, ruining her plan. Too few, and there won't be enough of them to tend to her eggs and larvae.

CUCKOO BUMBLEBEE

CUCKOO DUCK

Around 100 species of birds are brood parasites. Considering there are more than 11,000 species of birds in the world, that means the behavior is pretty rare! Only one duck does it—the black-headed duck of South America. The female secretly lays her eggs in the nests of other water birds, including various ducks and gulls.

BROWN-HEADED GULL

DUCK CHICK

GULL CHICK

BLACK-HEADED DUCK

LAY AND LEAVE

After dumping her eggs, the female black-headed duck makes herself scarce. Meanwhile, the host she has chosen incubates her eggs alongside its own. When the black-headed ducklings hatch, they are independent from day one and leave their adopted family behind. As with all cuckoos, they never meet their birth mother.

CUCKOO CATFISH

Many of Africa's cichlid fish brood their eggs and babies in their mouths. This gives cuckoo catfish their chance. The male and female cuckoo catfish find a breeding pair of cichlids, and lay and fertilize their eggs at the same time. When the mother cichlid scoops her eggs up, she picks up the cuckoo catfish eggs as well!

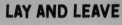

CICHLID FISH

73

DUCK-BILLED PLATYPUS

KNOCKOUT KICK

Very few mammals are venomous. One is Australia's duck-billed platypus, which is also odd for laying eggs and having a rubbery beak. There are hornlike prongs called spurs on the rear ankles of the male platypus. These give him a venomous kick! Victims say the pain is like being stung by hundreds of wasps. Luckily, the usual target is other male platypuses.

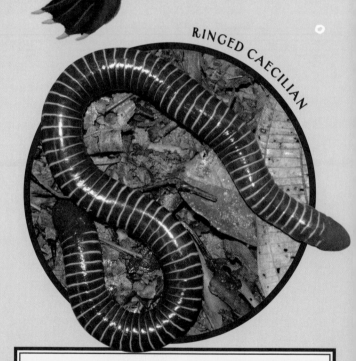

RINGED CAECILIAN

VENOM SURPRISE

Poison and venom work in a different way. You have to touch or eat a poisonous animal to be affected by its toxins. A venomous animal injects its prey with a sting or bite. Here are four of the most surprising venomous species.

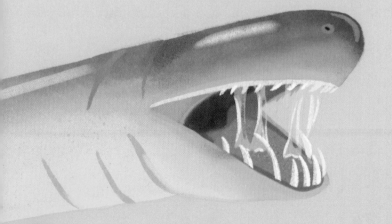

DOUBLE DEFENSE

Caecilians (you say their name "sih-sill-ee-ans") are perhaps the world's most bizarre amphibians. They look like large worms, can't see, and burrow through soil. The strange animals have TWO killer defenses. Their tails produce poison, while at the other end, their jaws contain venom glands. Venom is extremely rare in amphibians.

JAVAN SLOW LORIS

SWEAT AND SPIT

Among primates, the group of mammals to which monkeys and apes belong, just one species has venom—the Javan slow loris. It may look cute and cuddly, but its armpits are DEADLY. When it licks its sweat glands, the toxins mix with its saliva to make a venom that can rot flesh. The loris uses its venomous bite in fights with other lorises.

BRUNO'S CASQUE-HEADED FROG

KISS OF DEATH

Many frogs have poisonous skin for defense, but scientists did not think any were venomous...until now! In 2015, researchers discovered that two little frogs from Brazil do have venom. They deliver it with tiny bony spines on their lips. One of them, Bruno's casque-headed frog, has venom so powerful, just 0.04 oz (1 g) would be enough to kill 80 humans.

POISON DART FROG

POISONOUS PITOHUI

You can count the number of poisonous birds on the fingers of one hand. The first to be discovered by scientists was the hooded pitohui-but local people had always known its secret.

POTENT PLUMAGE

Don't mess with the hooded pitohui. (You say its name "pit-oh-wee.") Its feathers and skin are packed with poison-the same toxin as the one found in poison dart frogs in South America. The active ingredient is BTX, or batrachotoxin. This paralyzes muscles so the victim is unable to move, and can cause heart attacks and death.

DEADLY DIET

Like poison dart frogs, the hooded pitohui obtains its poison from its food. But no one is sure why it is poisonous. Maybe to fool predators? If so, the bird's orange-and-black coloration could be a warning. Several other species of birds in the area look similar to the pitohui-perhaps they deliberately mimic its appearance to keep themselves safe.

A hooded pitohui searches the forest for fresh fruit—its main food.

It notices a shiny, blue-and-yellow beetle and snaps it up. The beetle's toxins will come in very useful.

RED-SIDED GARTER SNAKE

People often mistakenly talk about "poisonous" snakes, when they really mean "venomous." Poison in snakes is incredibly rare! One of the few genuinely poisonous snakes is the red-sided garter snake from Canada and the USA. It picks up toxins from the newts it eats, and stores them in its body, which in turn makes it poisonous.

New Guinea has another poisonous bird: the blue-capped ifrita. And more may yet be found.

HOODED PITOHUI

PAINFUL LESSON

The first scientist to experience the hooded pitohui's defense was part of a team exploring the island of New Guinea in 1990. When he caught one briefly to study it, his hands began burning. People from this forested region call the species the "rubbish bird" for very good reason!

INDEX

ABOUT THE AUTHOR

BEN HOARE is a science writer and editor, and the author of the hugely successful *An Anthology of Intriguing Animals*, as well as *The Wonders of Nature, Nature's Treasures, The Secret World of Plants,* and *Weird and Wonderful Nature* for DK. He is passionate about nature and sharing his knowledge of the natural world.

ABOUT THE ILLUSTRATOR

ASIA ORLANDO is a digital artist, illustrator, and environmentalist. Asia creates artwork for books, magazines, products, and posters. Her work focuses on harmony between animals, humans, and the environment. She's also the founder of Our Planet Week, a social media event for illustrators aimed to address environmental issues.

ACKNOWLEDGMENTS

The publisher would like to thank the following for their kind permission to reproduce their photographs:

(Key: a-above; b-below/bottom; c-centre; f-far; l-left; r-right; t-top)

6 Dreamstime.com: Blagodeyatel (bl). **naturepl.com:** Pascal Kobeh (tc); Bruce Thomson (cr). **7 Alamy Stock Photo:** Ed Brown Wildlife (cr); Jared Hobbs / All Canada Photos (tc); Brian Parker (clb). **naturepl.com:** Eric Baccega (br). **8 Alamy Stock Photo:** Kumar Sriskandan (br). **Getty Images / iStock:** Searsie (cla). **9 Alamy Stock Photo:** Michael & Patricia Fogden / Minden Pictures (tc). **naturepl.com:** Konrad Wothe (cr). **10 Alamy Stock Photo:** Kirk Hewlett (br). **11 naturepl.com:** Mark Carwardine (t). **12-13 Alamy Stock Photo:** Sandesh Kadur / Nature Picture Library. **14 Alamy Stock Photo:** Mike Parry / Minden Pictures (c). **15 Alamy Stock Photo:** Claudio Contreras / Nature Picture Library (c). **16 Alamy Stock Photo:** David Mann (br). **naturepl.com:** Fred Bavendam (tl). **17 Alamy Stock Photo:** Chris Stenger / Buiten-Beeld (clb); Science History Images (tr); Kevin Schafer (c). **Dreamstime.com:** Nopadol Uengbunchoo (crb). **18 Shutterstock.com:** Narek87. **19 Alamy Stock Photo:** Mark Boulton (br). **20 Alamy Stock Photo:** Chris Mattison / Nature Picture Library (t). **21 Alamy Stock Photo:** Beth Watson / Stocktrek Images (b). **Science Photo Library:** L. Newman & A. Flowers (cl). **22 naturepl.com:** Klein & Hubert (t). **23 naturepl.com:** Terry Whittaker (r). **24 Alamy Stock Photo:** Dan Sullivan (cr). **25 naturepl.com:** Richard Du Toit. **26 Alamy Stock Photo:** Jonathan Mbu (Pura Vida Exotics) (tr). **naturepl.com:** Barry Mansell (bl). **27 Dreamstime.com:** Henner Damke (br). Trond H. Larsen: (tl). **28 Alamy Stock Photo:** David Tipling Photo Library (r). **29 Alamy Stock Photo:** Tui De Roy / Nature Picture Library (c). **30 Alamy Stock Photo:** Morgan Trimble (t). **31 naturepl.com:** Shane Gross (b). **32-33 Alamy Stock Photo:** Ryohei Moriya / Associated Press. **34 naturepl.com:** Luiz Claudio Marigo (c). **35 Alamy Stock Photo:** Stephen Belcher / Minden Pictures (c). **36 Alamy Stock Photo:** Suzi Eszterhas / Minden Pictures (cr); Survivalphotos (tl). **37 Alamy Stock Photo:** blickwinkel / Teigler (tr); Ch'ien Lee / Minden Pictures (br). **38 Alamy Stock Photo:** David Tipling Photo Library (c). **39 Alamy Stock Photo:** blickwinkel / A. Hartl (c). **40-41 Jason Penney. 40 Alamy Stock Photo:** Valentin Wolf / imageBROKER.com GmbH & Co. KG (bc). **41 Tom Keener:** (cr). **42 Alamy Stock Photo:** Cyril Ruoso / Nature Picture Library (tr). **43 Alamy Stock Photo:** Thomas Marent / Minden Pictures. **44 Alamy Stock Photo:** Richard Revels / Nature Photographers Ltd (b). **45 Alamy Stock Photo:** Larry Doherty (t). **46 Alamy Stock Photo:** Alf Jacob Nilsen (tr); Eng Wah Teo (cl). **47 Alamy Stock Photo:** blickwinkel / AGAMI / V. Legrand (cr); Gabbro (cl). **49 NGA Manu Nature Reserve. 50 Alamy Stock Photo:** Neil Bowman (r). **51 Alamy Stock Photo:** Sebastian Kennerknecht / Minden Pictures (c). **52 Alamy Stock Photo:** amana images inc. (tl); Richard Becker (crb). **53 Alamy Stock Photo:** blickwinkel / H. Bellmann / F. Hecker (bl). **Shutterstock.com:** Agnieszka Bacal (cr). **54-55 Alamy Stock Photo:** blickwinkel / Hartl (t). **56 Alamy Stock Photo:** Stephane Granzotto / Nature Picture Library (b). **57 BluePlanetArchive.com:** Jeremy Stafford-Deitsch (t). **58 Alamy Stock Photo:** Remo Savisaar (c). **59 Alamy Stock Photo:** Daniel Heuclin / Nature Picture Library (crb);

VPC Animals Photo (c). **60 Alamy Stock Photo:** cbimages (cra). naturepl.com: Dave Watts (br). **61 123RF.com:** feathercollector (cb). **Alamy Stock Photo:** Heather Angel / Natural Visions (tl). **63 Alamy Stock Photo:** Christian Ziegler / Danita Delimont, Agent (cra); Suzi Eszterhas / Minden Pictures (l). **64-65 Science Photo Library:** Gregory Dimijian (t). **65 naturepl.com:** Neil Bromhall (cra). **66 Alamy Stock Photo:** imageBROKER / Emanuele Biggi (c). **67 Alamy Stock Photo:** Jerry and Marcy Monkman / EcoPhotography.com (c); Jared Hobbs / All Canada Photos (cr). **68 Ardea:** Paulo de Oliveira (tr); Paulo Di Oliviera (cl). **69 Alamy Stock Photo:** Franco Banfi / Nature Picture Library (br). **Getty Images / iStock:** Yelena Rodriguez Mena (cl). **70-71 Alamy Stock Photo:** Anton Sorokin (t). **72 Alamy Stock Photo:** Will Watson / Nature Picture Library (b). **73 Dreamstime.com:** Gabriel Rojo (c). **74 Alamy Stock Photo:** D. Parer & E. Parer-Cook / Minden Pictures (tl); Pete Oxford / Minden Pictures (cr). **75 Alamy Stock Photo:** Andrew Walmsley / Nature Picture Library (tl). **Shutterstock.com:** Leonardo Mercon (br). **76 Dreamstime.com:** Dirk Ercken (tl). **77 Alamy Stock Photo:** Daniel Heuclin / Biosphoto

Cover images: Front: Alamy Stock Photo: Tui De Roy / Nature Picture Library bl, Kevin Schafer / Minden Pictures br, Paul Bertner / Minden Pictures tl; **Dorling Kindersley:** Asia Orlando 2022 c; **naturepl.com:** Joel Sartore / Photo Ark tr; Back: **Alamy Stock Photo:** Beth Watson / Stocktrek Images br, Juan Carlos Munoz / Nature Picture Library tr, Alf Jacob Nilsen bl; **Dorling Kindersley:** Asia Orlando 2022 c; **naturepl.com:** Shane Gross tl

All other images © Dorling Kindersley

Ben would like to thank
The super-fabulous creative team at DK, who took on my idea for this book and turned it into something special. A huge round of applause to my editor Abi Maxwell, ably assisted by James Mitchem, and to the entire design team – Charlotte Milner, Sonny Flynn, Bettina Myklebust Stovne, and Brandie Tully-Scott. You are the best in the business!

Asia Orlando, you have brought such wit and joy to the book with your gorgeous illustrations. Your work makes the book sing. Thanks too to my lovely agent Gill for being so supportive.

Above all, I want to thank our mind-blowing variety of fellow earthlings. Some of these creatures may be odd, but they are all wonderful, and we're so lucky to share this planet with them.

DK would like to thank
Olivia Stanford for editorial assistance; Polly Goodman for proofreading; Helen Peters for indexing; Sakshi Saluja for picture research; and Roohi Rais for image assistance.